The *Global* Table

Celebrations and Contemporary Inspirations

Tatjana Schantz Johnsson

Words by Marión Bravo-Bhasin

Photography by Alan Lee and Edward Hendricks

mc **Marshall Cavendish** Editions

til Nikolas og Rebekka, kaerligst mor

Published by Marshall Cavendish Editions
An imprint of Marshall Cavendish International
1 New Industrial Road, Singapore 536196

Other Marshall Cavendish Offices:
Marshall Cavendish Ltd. 119 Wardour Street, London W1F OUW, UK • Marshall Cavendish Corporation. 99 White Plains Road, Tarrytown NY 10591-9001, USA • Marshall Cavendish International (Thailand) Co Ltd. 253 Asoke, 12th Flr, Sukhumvit 21 Road, Klongtoey Nua, Wattana, Bangkok 10110, Thailand • Marshall Cavendish (Malaysia) Sdn Bhd, Times Subang, Lot 46, Subang Hi-Tech Industrial Park, Batu Tiga, 40000 Shah Alam, Selangor Darul Ehsan, Malaysia

Marshall Cavendish is a trademark of Times Publishing Limited

National Library Board Singapore Cataloguing in Publication Data
Schantz Johnsson, Tatjana, 1969-
The global table : celebrations and contemporary inspirations / Tatjana Schantz Johnsson; text by Marión Bravo-Bhasin; photography by Alan Lee and Edward Hendricks. – Singapore : Marshall Cavendish Editions, c2006.
p. cm.
Includes index.
ISBN : 981-261-065-0

1. Table setting and decoration. 2. Entertaining. I. Bravo-Bhasin, Marión, 1964- II. Lee, Alan, 1959- III. Hendricks, Edward, 1960- IV. Title.

TX879
642.6 — dc21   SLS2005043474

Printed by Tien Wah Press (Pte) Ltd

Contents

Introduction

The idea for doing a book on global celebrations came to me soon after starting my career as a stylist. I discovered that I really enjoyed the assignments where I was asked to put together a 'non-traditional' looking table setting for say, Chinese New Year. I enjoyed learning about the customs and traditions and creatively, I loved the task of playing with all the elements you have on a table setting (plates, napkins, glassware etc…) and coming up with something original and inviting. I figured I was not alone.

But for the book I had in mind, one thing had to be present and dominant—the global aspect. The world is shrinking, boundaries are vanishing and it's becoming increasingly easier and easier to find beautiful, inexpensive ethnic items in major cities around the world. The global trend is here to stay and nowhere does it all come together more naturally and magnificently as on a dining table.

By highlighting 20 different cultural celebrations, my goal is to present them in a contemporary manner that will invite you to learn a little, to partake, to experiment and to enjoy the vast ethnic influences around us. More specifically, my intention is not to lay out a traditional looking Japanese table setting, but to show how you can be *inspired* by Japanese, English or Mexican celebrations and traditions to create a splendid table setting to suit your own entertaining needs. For instance, for the Scottish Burn's Night, why not invite your friends to bring a favourite poem (or haiku or sonnet or limerick) to share over dinner and drinks? It doesn't have to be a Burn's poem, it doesn't even have to be in January, but it certainly can be a fun evening for all!

The other unifying theme in this book is that food, family and friends always go together—no matter where you live. When you are lucky enough to have all these three elements, your efforts will always be rewarded when you take the time to make your table a place of beauty and a place where people are always welcomed.

While working on this book, several things started to become clear to me. One is how people from every walk of life seem to celebrate the same things e.g. light or the moon; how so many festivals and celebrations have merged and evolved from a blend of different cultures and religious influences; and how it all starts with one bit of inspiration. Within these pages I hope you will enjoy the trip around the world, discover some interesting traditions, ideas, inspiration and as a result, many memorable and enjoyable evenings will soon follow.

A Poetry Fling
Burn's Night

An evening shared with friends, filled with food, drink, music, dance and poetry—what could be more civilised? A true Scotsman probably doesn't need any special occasion to partake in any of the aforementioned; however, the rest of us could certainly borrow from the Scottish tradition of Burn's Night. If you've never hosted or participated in a 'Burns Supper', perhaps it's time to become acquainted with this celebratory, literary evening.

Inspired by the famed Scottish castles and rugged, impressive countryside, the earthy amber, ochre and wooden tones and natural materials create an ambience of relaxed elegance.

Whether the evening is formal and traditional or casual and fun-filled, the purpose is to pay tribute to a great Scotsman, Robert Burns. Strive to create an embracing atmosphere that will immediately make your guests feel at ease and transport them to Scotland. For the room, the aim is to create warmth and a castle-wise ambience. Earthy hues such as orange and gold liven up the dark wood table and project the feel of a cosy, glowing fire. Using soft textures such as feathers and fur at the place settings enhance the natural side of this mystical and lush land. For a bit of drama on the table, some space is devoted to a collection of shapely, sculptural vases—a tribute to the elusive Scottish legend of the Loch Ness monster.

To achieve a contemporary, yet unmistakably Scottish atmosphere, tartan print is used as an accent rather than the focal point. This material makes fitting napkins that don't overwhelm the place setting. Or even some easy-to-find tartan ribbon could be wrapped and tied around the glasses or cutlery for a whimsical touch. Lastly, plenty of soft candlelight, on and around the table, and the room will be instantly transformed into a welcoming Highland retreat.

The traditional end to any Burn's Night is the singing of the Bard's sentimental favourite, 'Auld Lang Syne'.

The Scottish piper is a stately figure, recognised the world over.

Different elements come together to give the full flavour of Scotland.

The mystery of Loch Ness is recalled with
this dramatic grouping of vases.

Include interesting, unexpected details such as this peacock.

Pheasant-feathered decorations are clipped onto napkin rings and decorate an imitation leather charger plate that sits comfortably on a piece of rabbit fur.

In honour of the life and works of Robert Burns, Scotland's most famous poet, special suppers have been held annually on his birthday for over 200 years. Born on 25 January 1759, 'The Bard' is renowned worldwide as a great poet and songwriter. A keen social commentator, Burns wrote poignantly about love, universal brotherhood and the human condition.

The Burn's Night supper tradition was started by close friends of the poet a few years after his death (in 1796) as a tribute to his memory. The basic format for the evening still follows the same pattern and purpose of honouring Scotland's Bard. The evening begins with the eating of a Scottish meal—haggis, mince, tatties and neeps (potatoes and rutabagas)—the liberal drinking of Scotch whisky and the recitation of Burn's songs and poetry. And, of course, the Piper is essential to pipe in the haggis and perhaps even get the Highland fling going after the meal!

Scotch whisky, or 'the water of life' as it's famously regarded by its loyal countrymen, is integral to the celebration.

Plush textures and warm tones are always inviting. Try to include a few tactile elements, such as this soft rabbit fur and beautifully grained cutlery, for added interest.

Add a modern twist to your reunion lunch.

Abundant Orange
Chinese Lunar New Year

It's all about luck, prosperity and abundance for the Chinese. This beguiling culture is known the world over for its use of good luck symbols, auspicious colours and intriguing superstitions. Think jade amulets, red and gold, yin and yang, to name just a few. Consequently, it comes as no surprise that during the Chinese Lunar New Year—the most important and longest holiday in China—customs, symbols and superstitions abound.

Today, the Chinese diaspora have brought their many traditions to every corner of the world. The first day of the lunar calendar which can fall anywhere between the last week of January and the first few weeks of February, is a cause for celebration to Chinese worldwide. Festivities traditionally last 15 days and were once the only time farmers took a break from working the fields. Stemming from China's agrarian origins, the New Year celebrations also marked the beginning of spring. The holiday has always hinged on, and continues to hinge on, family togetherness, reunions and harmony. In fact, throughout Asia, this festival is probably the most important one of the year. For the Vietnamese, Tet is the New Year. The Koreans celebrate Solnal and Losar is the Tibetan New Year.

The unique shape and colour of the five-generation plant makes it a favourite New Year decoration.

In this table setting, we choose to showcase the Lunar New Year with a modern twist. Traditionally, red and gold are the auspicious colours closely associated with the New Year; however, orange provides a refreshing nod to the celebration. The Cantonese word for oranges is identical to the word for 'gold' so kumquat plants are always present while oranges and mandarins are exchanged during the festivities as a symbol of wealth and abundance. Yet, one hardly sees the colour as the focal point of the table. Why not start a new tradition?

The garden setting, modern white table top and bold colours all contribute to an inviting family reunion lunch. The eye-popping centrepiece is another clever twist to a traditional favourite. The Solanum Mammosum, also known as the five-generation fruit, symbolises abundance. The plant always makes an appearance during the celebration (for its auspicious colour and the fact that the plant blossoms at this time of the year) and here, by filling two extra tall glass cylinders

with a couple of stems, the take is refreshing and beautiful. And photo/memo holders, made out of orange cables, display funky name cards cum *hong baos*—little red packets containing money that are given by adults to young people as an expression of good wishes and good fortune.

A natural partner for orange is gold. Here, it complements the orange and accents the table in the form of gold lacquer place mats and gold trimmed glasses. More luck!

By making a little effort with the background details, your table setting will be complete. A few colourful lanterns, hung strategically, dress up the lush surroundings. Even if your meal is indoors, a few paper lanterns will not be out of place. Hang them from the ceiling, above a window or simply rest them on top of a side table. The goal is to blend as many of the traditional aspects as possible while carefully incorporating a few new twists of one's own. In essence, a little rebirth and growth for all.

Chinese traditions offer plenty of symbols and good luck charms that bring fun to the occasion. Bring out the firecrackers in the form of candy to end your dinner 'with a bang'.

Gold-toned glasses, along with cheongsam and decorative bottle wraps, dress up the occasion.

Set your table with style and wit. It's fun and easy to incorporate some quirky details as long as you bear in mind your colour scheme and try to play off some other strong element. The round photo/ name card holders work wonderfully not only because of their orange colour but because they also echo the large round crystals on the table.

Oranges are always abundant during the celebration and are given and received in pairs upon entering a friend's or relative's home. Display them in a pretty container.

More Traditional Touches

- Plants and flowers symbolise rebirth and growth. Scatter vases and plants around your living space to create a welcoming atmosphere. Commonly used are plants such as plum blossoms, and flowers such as pussy willow, azalea, peony, water lily or narcissus. Bamboo is also known for its compatibility.
- Candy trays have more meaning than just satisfying your sweet tooth. A circular tray symbolises togetherness, while the goodies represent sweetness. Traditionally the tray has eight sides (the number eight is considered lucky in Chinese and seen as a symbol of prosperity) and is filled with goodies like red dates (which bring hope for prosperity), melon seeds (for proliferation) and cookies.

The Lion Dance and the Dragon Dance are always performed as part of the New Year celebrations to frighten away the bad spirits and to bring good luck and prosperity in the coming year.

Crystals are also believed to bring good luck. The large orange crystal decorations on the table beautifully complement the small crystal fish (representing abundance) decoration that playfully hangs on the stem of the wine glass.

Stake your claim on a romantic setting, whether it's on the beach, in the mountains or in your own backyard. The idea is to find what you like and make it your own special place for the occasion.

Island Love
Valentine's Day

This Valentine's Day—or better yet, any day—spark, rekindle or ignite the romance in your life with an extra romantic, simple beach setting for two. With a little sand between your toes, there is no need for any fuss or formality. Four poles and a billowy cloth establish your space and a small portable table and rattan stools create your eating area. The rest lies in the details and a little preparation.

With nature as your backdrop, keep the 'extras' simple and well thought out. Simple meaning romantic, of course! Several symbols of romance are universal and a little subtlety creates a clear message of love. Red and white serve as the important foundation. Flowers are de rigueur and roses are infamous for their gorgeous scent and association with romance and love. Other flowers that have long been considered romantic include daisies, violets and bachelor buttons. And then there is the heart. Nothing says love stronger or faster than does the heart symbol. Use these symbols sparingly or generously—the message is yours. Your mini-paradise is now complete, so relax and enjoy the breeze, sun, sky and, above all, your company.

A string of toile roses and red paper lanterns are another example of casual details that instantly make the celebration something special.

The simplicity of the flute-shaped vase enhances the beauty of the roses.

Jazz up some champagne flutes with red ribbon and paper hearts. Acrylic photo frames double as coasters, with some heart-shaped confetti inserted in the middle.

A few retro Hawaiian luau trays are ideal for a casual outdoor meal.

Enjoy life's simple pleasures.

The ultimate romantic ingredients—roses, chocolate and champagne.

Red, romantic details are everywhere. Incorporate whatever suits your style.

Every 14 February, in many countries, gifts, flowers and candy are exchanged between loved ones, all in the name of St. Valentine. But who was St. Valentine, and why all the fuss?

As with most ancient celebrations, the history of this romantic day is shrouded in mystery. Valentine's Day, as we know it today, contains traces of both Roman and Christian tradition. The celebration is said to originate from the Roman fertility festival called Lupercalia. A pagan festival, Lupercalia was held on 15 February. Before this day, boys would draw names of girls out of an urn and the couple would exchange gifts on the day of the festival.

In the 3rd century, a young Roman priest named Valentine served during the reign of Emperor Claudius II. The emperor ordered his Roman soldiers not to marry or become engaged because he believed that single men made better soldiers than those with wives and families. Valentine defied the Emperor's decree and secretly married the young couples. He was eventually arrested, imprisoned then put to death on 14 February. In AD 470, Lupercalia was given a Christian spin by the Pope when he declared that the festival would now be in honour of Valentine.

Although the truth behind the Valentine legends is muddled, the stories certainly emphasise his appeal as a sympathetic, heroic and, most importantly, romantic figure.

Kimono bottle wraps turn the ordinary drink into a Japanese treat.

Finely worked porcelain dolls capture the feminine essence of the occasion.

Japanese Blossoms
Hinamatsuri

This feminine table setting is inspired by Hinamatsuri, a festival that celebrates the growth and happiness of young girls. To create this Japanese-themed setting, a great starting point is a low table with beautiful Asian lines. Even a coffee table and cushions, dressed up with Japanese prints would be ideal since the occasion calls for young guests. Keeping to a pastel colour scheme of pink and baby blue, and adding the requisite peach blossom and other floral prints, is sure to delight your girls and reinforce the spirit of the celebration.

Take further inspiration from Japan's unmatched appreciation and interpretation of nature as expressed in their tableware, kimonos, flower arrangements and rock gardens, for example. Try to weave in this 'nature' inspiration in the form of flowers, pottery, handmade cards and even antique or modern textiles for a truly authentic, rich feel to your table.

As with any celebration, food is an integral element that allows for self-expression. Serve what you like and what will please your guests. There are, however, a few dishes that, for most Japanese, are synonymous with the festival—red, white and green triangular-shaped sticky rice cakes (*hishi-mochi*); sweet white sake (*shiro-zake*) and sugar-coated popped rice crackers (*hina-arare*). Interestingly, the colour of these foods are also symbolic of March and the seasonal changes that occur during this time: green represents the new shoots or sprouting plants, pink the peach blossoms and white the snow.

A few time-honoured Japanese traditions also lend themselves beautifully to this setting. The 'dry garden' or Kanshoniwa is quite easy to make in miniature at home. A simple square tray with fine sand, a few smooth rocks and a small rake is all that is needed to make an endless canvas. In addition, a small origami figure instantly enhances a set of chopsticks. It takes expertise to make the delicate fish ornament in the setting (these were bought in a stationary store) but origami can offer lots of entertainment as an activity to the celebration.

Japanese earthenware comes in every price range and colour. Buy what you love and it's bound to complement each other in the end.

Flower petals scattered over handmade paper creates an attractive setting that will delight your guests.

Femininity defined. The fluorescent pink sash is actually a young girl's obi.

Dragonfly chopstick rests make a simple statement but a lasting impression.

The bare essentials of Japanese tableware. These delicate origami fish are from a stationary store but making origami figures can also be a great activity for your invitees.

More feminine Japanese touches.

A young girl's kimono is simply too beautiful to keep hidden away. Even her shoes are a showpiece of their own.

The simple beauty of the ancient Zen gardens still hold true today.

Kimonos are beautiful showpieces of nature settings.

Pretty greeting cards come in all kinds of handmade paper designs and colours. Find some that you can't resist and use them not only for giving but also as display items in bird cages, as coasters, as backgrounds to create a little 'still-life', whatever your mood dictates.

Celebrated on 3 March since the Edo Period (1603–1867), Hinamatsuri or Doll Festival is an occasion to pray for a young girl's growth, health and happiness. The boy's festival or children's day (Kodomo-no-hi) is celebrated on 5 May. 'Hina' signifies a special type of Japanese doll and 'matsuri' means festival. Japan has a rich tradition of dolls that have served to protect the owners from harm by 'absorbing' the evil and consequently making it easier for the owner to deal with the unknown forces of nature. In ancient times, dolls were either worn close to the body or kept in the family shrine. The festival dates back to the ancient Chinese practice of transferring one's sins and misfortunes from the human body to a doll, and washing them away by setting the doll on a river to drift away.

In more modern times, the Hinamatsuri dolls (also known as Ohinasama) began to be displayed most commonly on a five- or seven-tiered hierarchical stepped display stand draped in red cloth, set to recreate a scene in a royal wedding. The top tier is where the Emperor and Empress sit in full attire. Next came three ladies in waiting, representing purity and beauty. Then the protectors of the court—the young warriors symbolise man's virility and prime while the older warriors represent experience and wisdom. The fourth tier is for the musicians—three drummers, a flute player and a singer— who represent the lighter side of life in all its gaiety. Second to last stand the three court vassals: one carrying shoes, one carrying an umbrella and the other refreshments. And

lastly, the tier for fine miniatures in furniture, utensils and often even an ox cart (the vehicle for nobles). All these dolls and miniatures are passed on from generation to generation. To this day, these beautiful, precious dolls are highly treasured and never regarded as toys. There is an old wives' tale that says that the display must be dismantled soon after 3 March or the young girl is destined to marry late in life.

This spring time festival is also known as the Momo-no-sekku or Peach Festival because the peach blossoms come into all their glory during this month. This beautiful white bloom represents the feminine traits of gentility, composure and tranquillity and is also closely associated with a happy marriage.

An eclectic and colourful mix of inspiration.

An Amazon Table
Carnival

Being that Brazil is a tropical country, delicious and exotic fruit is part of everyday life. Brazilians love to decorate with it and a colourful tray of ripened, aromatic fruit creates an enticing display that can later be enjoyed by all.

If you want to host a Carnival party, have one phrase in mind—over the top. It's the time to have fun, dance in the streets, let your inhibitions down and party with enthusiasm.

To recreate the energy and dazzle of the festivities, we staged a table as ornate as any float in the Samba Parade. A mannequin bust dressed up in butterfly wings, feather headdress, boa plumes and a Venetian-style mask sets the dress code. It seems like the festivities have always been about the mixing of the social classes, and with costumes and masks, this was easily achieved. Today of course, costumes and headgear have taken on an entirely new direction, but the spirit of dressing up and enjoying oneself continue to be present. After all, Carnival is not about restraint!

The mix of colours, shiny surfaces, glitter, sequins, ornate miniature masks and cut-coloured stemware make for a celebratory setting, sure to ignite any evening. Cover the table with decoration on the plates, in the glasses—even the back of the chairs can be adorned with large masks! Take a close inspection of your Christmas decorations and you probably already have a good start with the table ornaments: strands of coloured beads and baubles, glittery fruit; even the mini feathered bustier was initially an ornament that gets a 'second showing' by simply removing the hanging string.

Once you have a party theme in mind, you will be amazed at how much inspiration is out there if you know where to look. Miniature Venetian-style masks and bejewelled eye masks are worth searching out in party supply stores and whenever the holiday decorations begin to arrive.

If you have ever seen the real Samba Parade or a clip of the festivities, you'll understand the glitz, shine, showmanship and spectacular costumes that are the centre of the celebration. Work with these adjectives in mind and your party table will easily recreate the razzle-dazzle of Carnival.

Your place is set for a fun evening. A brilliant eye mask greets guests while coloured stemware and drink umbrellas create the festive atmosphere.

Found at a party supply store, these large sun-inspired masks are a perfect fit for the dining-table chairs.

Beautifully cut, ruby-coloured stemware hold their own perfectly against the vibrant palette and details on the table.

Carnival is a four-day Christian celebration that begins on a Saturday and ends on Fat Tuesday, or Mardi Gras. Carnival Sunday is seven weeks before Easter Sunday, usually falling in February, sometimes March. The origins of this ancient celebration seem unclear but it can be traced back to pre-Christian times, to the spring celebrations in ancient Babylonia, Greece, Egypt and Rome. In those days, the festivities were a unique time to blur the lines between the social classes, aided by fancy masks and disguises—slaves dined with their masters in an atmosphere of decadence and excess. Later, in the Middle Ages, the Catholic Church assimilated Carnival into the Christian calendar as the last celebration before Lent (the 40-day period prior to Easter that the Christian church observes as a time of penance). The word 'carnival' is said to originate from the Latin *carnem levare* (to remove meat) or the Italian *carne vale* (a farewell to meat).

This festival is celebrated with abandon all over the world— Nice, France; New Orleans, Louisiana; Binche, Belgium and Venice, Italy all host world-famous festivities—but Rio de Janeiro's Carnaval (in Portuguese) is arguably the largest of the pre-Lenten festivals and a huge source of national pride and showmanship for the Brazilians. The famous Samba Parade began in the 1930s and today, Samba schools practise all year to perform and compete in the spectacular show that is broadcast to dozens of countries all around the world.

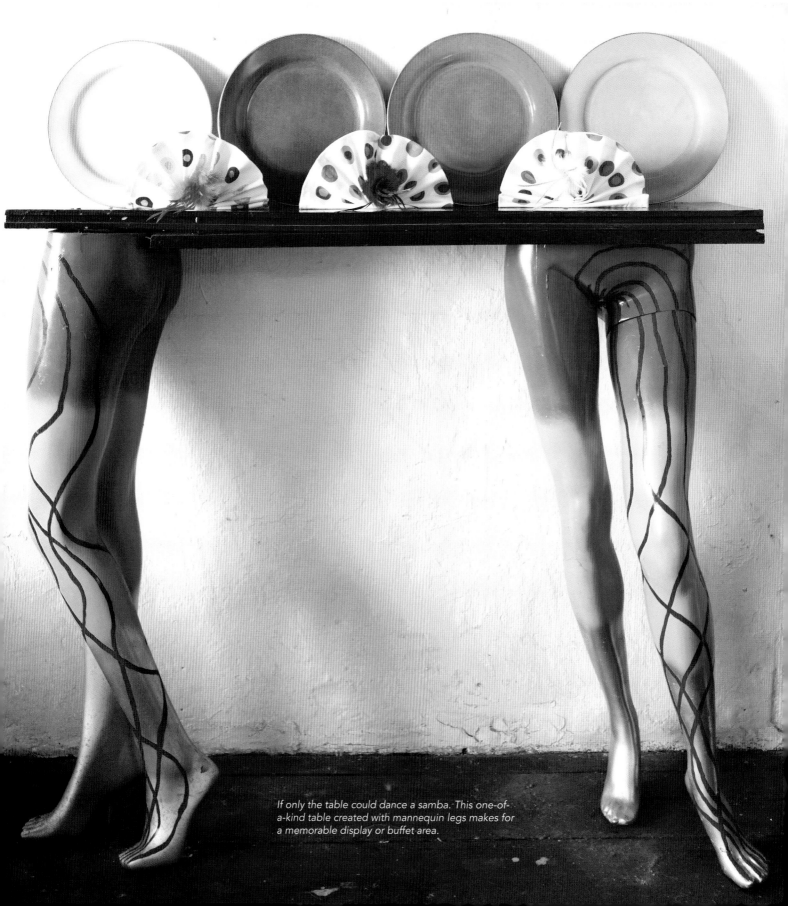

If only the table could dance a samba. This one-of-a-kind table created with mannequin legs makes for a memorable display or buffet area.

A Venetian carnival decoration dresses up the place-setting.

Think plumes, boas and beads if you want to create instance glamour and razzle-dazzle.

An Irish Jig and a Jug
St. Patrick's Day

The table is set—please join us.

'May your blessings outnumber the shamrocks that grow
And may trouble avoid you wherever you go.'

—Irish Blessing

St. Patrick's Day is a fascinating celebration. It's hard to think of another holiday so closely connected to one country where, worldwide and whatever your heritage, suddenly on 17 March, everyone celebrates all things Irish. It's not a spectator holiday. All that is required is an Irish pub, or at the very least, a cold glass of Guinness, and a few acquaintances. In some cities in the United States, there are major parades, rivers are dyed a shade of emerald hue and classrooms of children are dressed in green. In Ireland, it is a very important religious holiday that commemorates not just the patron saint of Ireland but is also a holiday to celebrate rich Irish traditions.

With Ireland's famous lush rolling countryside and shamrocks as the 'national flower', it is almost impossible to not have a green colour theme if you want an Irish table setting. By mixing a few purple and grey accents with a fresh tone of green, the feel is very modern and striking. Adding immensely to this contemporary look is the understated beauty and contrasting tone of the chengai wood and stainless steel table.

This long, narrow table is ideal for showcasing a series of arrangements throughout its length. Fields of shamrocks are recreated by joining four heart-shaped containers (florist's oasis—the styrofoam-like material that is used for floral arrangements—often comes in

heart shapes), studding them with green, silk rosebuds and displaying these on artificial grass mats. This simple eye-catcher reflects some of that Irish fun and wit. The other centrepiece is, of course, the tall green beer bottles.

Another great way to insert some creativity is with the cutlery presentation. Continuing with the green and nature theme, a small piece of artificial grass, cut into a rectangle and rolled around the silverware, is held in place with a piece of green cord—easy and fun.

St. Patrick's Day is that perfect incentive to invite some friends and have some fun. No formalities are required; just a lot of Irish spirit and hospitality.

Another detail well worth the trouble is painting green some wooden letters that can be found at art stores. They easily stand up with a little Blu-tack™ and cleverly help to define the occasion.

A few smooth stones spray-painted in gold touches on two famous Irish symbols—the Blarney stone and the pot of gold.

No Irish evening is complete without some of the popular after-dinner traditions of singing and doing a little jig or dance. When the time is right, bring out a simply decorated container of Irish blessings, toasts and/or songs to keep the evening going. Since shamrocks may be difficult to find in some areas, just think of them as four small hearts. By removing the stems of green, heart pins and hot gluing them onto the paper, you have an original seal.

45

Another bit of whimsy for the table—
wrap the cutlery in a small piece of
artificial grass and knot them together
with a grass-like cord.

It is difficult to separate the history of St. Patrick from myths and legends. Originally named Maewyn, St. Patrick was born in Wales towards the end of the 4th century AD. At the age of 16, he was taken prisoner from his home by Irish raiders and sold into slavery in Ireland. While in captivity, he believed he was visited by an angel and had a vision of converting people to Christianity. After six years of forced labour, he escaped and entered a monastery where he took the name Patrick. He studied at a monastery for 12 years before returning to Ireland to convert his former captors to Christianity. A remarkably effective missionary, he established numerous monasteries and schools during his time. St. Patrick preached in Ireland until his death, 30 years later, on 17 March 461.

One of the many legends surrounding St. Patrick is that he used a three-leaf shamrock to illustrate the doctrine of the Holy Trinity—the Father, Son and Holy Spirit—three entities all with the same origin, symbolised by the centre stem. Many people believe the shamrock came to be the traditional symbol of Ireland as a result of this legend.

Ireland certainly has its share of myths and symbols; incorporating a few such as this 'pot of gold', to your evening will ensure plenty of fun.

The straight lines and symmetry project a clean contemporary look.

A Modern Renaissance
Easter

*A 'moveable feast'—the sleek, functional
table is on wheels, and if so desired,
can be easily moved near the seating
area to accommodate more guests.*

This Easter celebration is inspired by bold hues and clean, modern design. Modern design for a modern renaissance, one could say. And where does design, renaissance and Easter all come together beautifully? Italy, of course.

Being that Easter falls on a Sunday, it's the perfect holiday to have a 'rejuvenating' brunch at home with family and friends. For an informal brunch, you can stack and cluster chunky dishes and glasses for guests to help themselves. And setting the food out in decorative, simple

Decorative, simple vessels allow guests to serve themselves with ease.

On your travels, keep your eyes open for pretty handmade ornaments and decorations. Propped against clean, modern dishes and surfaces, they add much visual interest.

Chinese hand-painted enamel makes a comeback and functions as a lovely yet inexpensive tray.

Simple white porcelain will never let you down.

A jewel-bright Easter brunch.

serving dishes will further encourage your guests to take what they want with ease and frequency.

Try interspersing a few interesting pieces for added visual appeal and function. A small hand-painted coffee grinder matches the lilac napkins, amusing egg holders entice the diners, and even granny's enamel tray makes an appearance.

And, of course, the one universal symbol for life and rebirth that no Easter table can be without is the egg. Here we use it freely, hung as little wooden decorations from the candelabra, hand-painted and arranged on a cake stand, as drink stirrers and even sprinkled among the orange slices.

Even the chandelier gets accessorised with long strings of glass beads and richly coloured butterfly crystals.

A crystal cake stand with a store-bought feather boa and decorated Easter eggs help to create a soft and symbolic centrepiece. Even at brunch time, a tall classic candelabra is an elegant display.

A trio of Asian-inspired, painted flasks make for an original and cheerful flower arrangement.

Look for interesting ways to display napkins and name cards. Insert them in plain glasses then jazz them up with Easter-time motifs for a quick and easy look.

52

Painted ostrich eggs enhanced with velvet ribbon become show-stopping decorations.

Easter, the holiest of all Christian festivals, is a joyous time of rebirth, rejuvenation and rejoicing. It is a time to celebrate the resurrection of Jesus from the dead after his crucifixion. Easter Day is always on the Sunday following Good Friday and can fall anytime between 22 March and 25 April of the Gregorian calendar, depending on the lunisolar calendar.

In olden times, the ancient Saxons would celebrate spring and honour Eostre, the goddess of offspring and springtime. By chance, the pagan festival of Eostre happened at the same time as the Christian observance of the Resurrection of Christ. Eventually the festivals merged and the name was changed to the modern spelling of Easter. However, in many other languages (e.g. Latin, Greek, Danish, Dutch, Finnish, French, Italian, Portuguese, Russian, Scottish and Spanish), the holiday's name is derived from Pesach, the Hebrew name of Passover, a Jewish holiday to which it is closely linked.

In a predominately Catholic country like Italy, Easter is steeped in tradition and rituals. The celebration always revolves around the church, family, food and friends. Villages have symbolic processions called *via cruces* (literally, 'way of the cross') that recall the death and passion of Christ. Even major cities like Rome and Florence take on a new face and spirit with the arrival of spring. And of course, the most solemn and holy tradition of all is the Easter Mass presided over by the Pope and given to the thousands of pilgrims who gather every year at St. Peter's Square at the Vatican.

Let the Water Flow
Songkran Festival

Decorative fish ornaments adorning the plants extend the theme to the surroundings.

Techni-coloured food is a daily part of Thai life. Display the snacks in equally bright boxes, such as these bian dang ban (tiffin) style lunch containers, for sure-fire temptation. And some nifty name cards made out of colour-coordinated soap bars and large clips add a touch of fun.

A few crystals in the fish bowl provide just a hint of glisten and interest, and pop out against the fresh bamboo stick mat below.

With a few well thought-out details, it's easier than you may think to make an inviting setting worthy of all the Thai splendour and beauty. Thailand is chockfull of gorgeous symbols, shapes and colour inspirations. By incorporating a few of these elements, it is not difficult to recreate the ambience for a splendid Thai evening.

For this Songkran celebration or Thai New Year, the primary inspiration is water—not only represented by the poolside setting and fish bowls, but also by the azure blue cushions, place mats and decorative umbrella.

Water plays a vital role in the festivities as it is symbolic of the cleansing ritual and signifies purity.

To complement the azure blue, the pinks and purples of the lotus and orchid flowers found throughout Thailand are a natural choice. The lotus flower, so closely associated with Buddhism, plays a dominant role on the table in the form of tea light holders and decorations on each soup spoon. Orchids, readily available and affordable in many countries nowadays, are durable enough to de-stem and can be sprinkled casually on the table

and in the swimming pool for an irresistible indulgence.

As far as colours are concerned, it's good to take a lesson from the Thai people who have no fear of vibrant hues and bold, fantastic combinations. Just think of the deep hues of Thai silk, the ornate Buddhist temples or the vibrantly colourful flower markets. Try to work with at least two or three shades to make a modern mix.

And don't forget to keep nearby plenty of lanterns, candles and matches so you will be adequately prepared for dusk and a long, enjoyable evening.

The bright colours and strong shapes speak for themselves—cool, modern and fun.

Pouring scented water onto the hands of elders is a common practice during the festivities.

A cool drink by the pool is always inviting while plenty of lanterns are both practical and pleasing to the eye.

Bloom upon bloom, upon bloom. A striking, graphic place mat is used to full effect when teamed with a stack of glass dinnerware and additional lotus and orchid flowers.

A window flower box takes on a new role as a practical display for refreshments. With such a wide selection of drinks and chic packaging on the market, why not include a few into your celebration for quick, instant style?

Few countries can match the sheer number of festivals and holidays on the Thai calendar. Celebrations run the spectrum from Buddhist, royal or national, to new rituals, ancient rites or turning imported celebrations Thai. Regardless, the Thais' *sanuk* or their love for 'having fun' is fully unleashed at each occasion. And of course, as with all Thai celebrations, decorum and reverence are always at the core.

Of all the Thai celebrations and holidays, Songkran or the Thai New Year, is by far the largest and most popular of all festivities. Celebrated in mid-April, this ancient Buddhist celebration was adapted from India via Myanmar. In fact, the word 'Songkran' comes from Sanskrit and means 'to move into', or more specifically, refers to the beginning of a new solar year when the sun moves into Aries.

Songkran is also observed in Myanmar, Laos and Cambodia.

Apart from marking a new beginning, Songkran is also a time for giving thanks. It is an occasion for family reunions and paying respect. The underlying significance of Songkran is the process of cleansing and purification—the purging of all ills, misfortune and evil and the starting of the new year afresh with all that is good and pure. Water is the key element in this cleansing process.

The celebration has many ancient customs and traditions which are principally performed to bring good luck and prosperity. On the eve and first day of Songkran, various activities are completed to 'send off' the outgoing year. Spring-cleaning, personal cleansing and rituals as well

as offerings are all part of this renewal process. Over the next two days, Buddha images are bathed as part of the ceremony. Young people pour scented water into the hands of elders and parents as a sign of respect. Meeting friends and sprinkling water on each others' shoulders and hands is an act of wishing good luck. Offerings are made to Buddhist monks, and sand is brought to the temples for the building of sand castles which are then decorated with colourful flags and flowers.

In recent years, this tradition of sprinkling water has been exploited by overzealous Thais and tourists, and a huge water fight ensues in the streets of Thailand. The positive result is that this is a good way to beat the heat in what is normally the hottest month of the year!

The lotus flower-shaped centrepiece glows beautifully by night.

The serenity of Buddha enhances any setting.

A small chalkboard serves as a perfect menu display.

Lotus flowers, orchids and water lilies make for a tranquil side arrangement.

Your Southern Belle
Mother's Day

Who doesn't dream of breakfast in bed? With this small gesture and a few thoughtful touches, your mother will never enjoy a more pleasant wake-up call on her special day.

To create a beautiful tray, it's important to keep a few things in mind. First, select a tray that will complement either the room's décor or go with one that will complement a special theme or interest your mom loves. For this tray, the colour inspiration comes from the gorgeous custom-made silk cushions on the bed. The floral prints and intricate detailing surrounding the bed are reminiscent of a Victorian time and southern comforts. This only serves to enhance the soft and feminine side of the person being honoured on this occasion.

Breakfast beckons Mom to linger in bed on her special day.

Secondly, the beverage—a beautifully sculpted carafe and matching cup make for a spectacular presentation for that hot cup of coffee or tea. Thirdly, don't forget some flowers and a glass of champagne to start the day off right. And lastly, for a true celebration, include some tall thin candles inserted in a glass vase. Here, the candles are inserted in sugar but you can also use coloured sand, marbles, pebbles—whatever goes with your theme.

Your present could also be part of the presentation. Our gifts are wrapped in wood-panelled shelf paper to echo the tones of the wooden breakfast tray. Working with shelf paper requires some precision and patience, but the idea is to look in unexpected places for wrapping inspirations. Even the 'ribbon' can be original—silk flowers, lace, twine or beaded string.

Cheerful colours and candles will bring a smile to Mom's face.

Floral details inspire the colour theme of the breakfast tray. *Artistically wrapped presents are almost too pretty to open.*

It's interesting to note that the tradition of paying tribute to one's mother has been around since ancient times, although the emphasis has shifted throughout the centuries from honouring one, sole mother figure and even the 'Mother Church' to one's own mother. The ancient Greeks originated the tradition by throwing a special spring celebration for their mother, Rhea, wife of Cronus and the Mother of the Gods and Goddesses. The Romans had a similar festival for Cybele, their mother goddess.

Much later, during the 1600s, England celebrated a day called 'Mothering Sunday' on the fourth Sunday of Lent. This special day originally honoured the mothers of England, but as Christianity began to spread throughout the country, the celebration evolved to pay homage to the 'Mother Church'. Over the years, this church festival blended with Mothering Sunday and people celebrated this day as a mark of respect to their mothers as well as the church. Domestic workers living away from their families were often encouraged to return home and spend the day with their mother. There was even a special cake, called 'mothering cake', associated with the celebration.

In the United States, a Mother's Day for Peace was first suggested in 1872 by Julia Ward Howe as a day dedicated to peace. This celebration was held successfully for about 30 years. In 1907, Anna Jarvis, began a campaign to establish a national Mother's Day on the anniversary of her mother's death. The campaign was successful when, in 1914, U.S. President Woodrow Wilson, made Mother's Day a national holiday to be held each year on the second Sunday of May.

While many countries around the world celebrate their own Mother's Day at different times of the year, some countries such as Denmark, Finland, Italy, Turkey, Australia and Belgium also celebrate it on the second Sunday in May.

African King
Father's Day

This Father's Day table setting is defined by the classic partnership of black and white. Taking our cue from the unique white table, a striking urban safari is recreated. Black and white is a combination that is uniquely bold and understated, graphic and clean. Inspired by these adjectives and the singular, graphic beauty of a herd of zebras on the African savannahs, the setting is perfect for a king. The charcoal-tiled wall, the glowing teardrop light overhead and the modern fondue set at the centre of the table all work together to transport the guests on this special safari.

When the table is small, everything—the materials, its scale, texture and colours—will be immediately noticed and gain importance. Make everything count. The modern fondue set not only serves the meal but also functions as a memorable centrepiece in its own right. Stainless steel complements the zebra patterns while adding its own characteristic gleam. The inlaid stripe on the custom fibreglass table is both discreet and bold, while the toy zebra animals and artist's dummy add instant appeal and softness to this graphic table. Yet, even the artist's dummy is no ordinary mannequin. Plain wooden dummies were painted white and the zebra stripes were added with a black marker. This can be a fun project for the children and a special souvenir of the celebration. Finishing things off are chequered bandanas used as napkins and place mats cut out of wire netting.

Everything is well planned and stylish, something most Dads will appreciate and value.

A unique mosaic-tiled flower pattern creates a notable backdrop to this pared down setting.

The ubiquitous 1960s fondue set makes it to the new millennium with a strong, clean design and stainless steel exterior. Demanding centre stage, a fondue is always a great communal meal.

A racing chequered flag works perfectly as a napkin, with place mats cut from wire netting.

The camouflage effect injects plenty of fun to the table.

An urban take on the African safari.

Dads still love their toys. With a strong colour theme and pattern, gift ideas may be easier to come by than expected!

Father's Day came about in the United States through one woman's determination to honour her father for his selflessness and strength. Sonora Dodd's own father was widowed when his wife died in childbirth and he was left to raise their six children by himself on a rural farm in Washington. It was only after Mrs Dodd became an adult that she realised the strength and courage her father had shown in bringing up his children as a single parent. In 1909, she was inspired to establish a day dedicated to fathers after listening to a mother's day sermon. A year later, the first Father's Day was observed. In 1924, President Calvin Coolidge supported the idea of a national Father's Day but it would be another 42 years, in 1966, before President Lyndon B. Johnson signed a proclamation declaring the third Sunday of June as Father's Day.

In Canada, the United Kingdom and the United States, this special day for fathers is celebrated on the third Sunday in June every year. In Australia, however, Father's Day is celebrated on the first Sunday in September.

When it comes to infusing some fun, the uncommon is a sure pleaser. Zebras on the table, tipsy striped men, why not?

No-fuss stainless steel cups and bowls are remarkably versatile, durable and stylish.

Bull and Table
Pamplona Bull Run

Some people may dream of having the real-life thrill and experience to 'run with the bulls' but it's probably safe to say that the majority of people would be equally thrilled, if not more, to simply participate in a tastefully prepared Spanish-themed evening at home.

The starting point to this dramatic setting is the red lacquer table. Of course, not many of us may have a red dining-room table but a tablecloth, place mats or even long strips of coloured paper will instantly transform any surface into that perfect working canvas. To complement the red base, black was a natural choice for a 'bullish' event.

Using the bull as a source of creative ideas, witty touches such as the painted animal horns and satin ribbon that has been tied and zigzagged on the back of the chairs (symbolising the animal's movements) make for a unique addition to the setting. Even the black leather place mats and horn-style folded napkins take on new meaning.

For the centrepiece, the square table's width dictated something large and low so the guests can easily see and converse across the table. The unconventional floral centrepiece was inspired by the polka-dotted red and black Sevillana flamenco dresses. Charcoal adds textural interest to the arrangement while the durability and waxy surface of red anthuriums contributes to the drama; but red carnations, roses or your favourite flower would be equally effective. Small sculptural, ceramic black birds lend just another element of intrigue.

Since the Bull Run is such a male-oriented event, a few feminine touches in the shape of lace and hand fans help to balance out the evening. To create a unique decanter for the occasion, a wine bottle was stripped of its labels, a piece of lace (cut from an inexpensive plastic lace tablecloth) was glued on and then the entire bottle was spray painted black. Extra details such as these are well worth the effort for they truly make memorable and beautiful additions to your festivities.

72

Small animal horns (which were painted black) were found in a second-hand store. However, you can also make some fantastic imitations out of construction paper by just folding paper into cone shapes.

This unconventional centrepiece is inspired by the polka-dotted red and black Sevillana flamenco dresses. With a wide and large setting, it is best to keep the centrepiece low so guests can easily see and converse across the table.

The matador is perhaps the strongest Spanish symbol of courage and strength.

Stick to your red and black colour theme for all your table accessories and everything will blend and look elegant.

Details such as these hand fans are simple, pleasing and contribute immensely to creating the Spanish atmosphere that you are striving for.

As always, napkins are a great and easy way to add creativity to any table. Learning a few different folds and styles will give an instant lift to any setting.

Red floral glasses complement the lace bottles.

Spain's tradition and expertise with lace inspired the decoration of these wine bottles.

Spain's famous 'Pamplona Bull Run' or as it is officially known, Fiesta de San Fermín, is an immensely exciting and world famous festival that encapsulates the best of Spanish traditions. The present nine-day festival that starts on 6 July has a long and twisted history dating back to the 13th and 14th centuries. In short, three different events converged to form the current day fiesta. Firstly, there were the San Fermín (patron saint of bakers, wine merchants and cobblers) religious celebrations which have taken place in October for centuries. Secondly, commercial fiestas, Feria del Toro, and bullfights have taken place in July since the Middle Ages. Thirdly, there was the Fiesta of San Juan on 24 June that would last 20 days. Through the years, these three fiestas merged and the Town Council requested the bishop to shift the celebration to 7 July (which currently begins at noon on 6 July). Consequently, in 1590, the Fiesta de San Fermín was born. And of course, there is Ernest Hemingway to thank who, in 1926, wrote about the Fiesta in *The Sun Also Rises* and encouraged people from all over the world to come and live for themselves the emotions he describes in the novel.

The Running of the Bulls, or the Encierro, originated out of a necessity to transfer the bulls from their corral outside of town to the bullring, in town. In the beginning, young men from the town would gather along the way to watch the action, and soon people started to join in to help. Although, Pamplona isn't the only Spanish town to hold a 'running of the bulls', it is by far the largest and most famous.

Fiesta!
Birthday Party

Irresistable, bold Mexican colours.

Colourful sweets in fun containers are instant party makers.

Birthday gatherings are joyous, happy occasions around the world for young and old alike. When staging a child's birthday, the energy and vibrancy of bright colours are impossible to ignore and overlook. Throw in a Mexican theme and you have every right to play with the rainbow!

In Mexico, like in all of Latin America, a child's birthday party is also a family affair. Relatives of all ages, distant cousins, everyone who is near and able to attend the party will certainly make an appearance.

Noise and fun, food and dance—it all comes together spontaneously in Latin America, when family is together.

As the focal point, a colourful Mexican serape (also known as Saltillo style) cotton blanket transforms into a festive tablecloth. If you do not own a Mexican blanket, no worries; any bright primary-coloured cloth or tablecloth will work equally well. To add more shades to the table, alternate intensely coloured plates that match the tablecloth. And different

shaped stemware will add even more visual appeal.

Even though you may not begin your meal with watermelon, there is no denying how spectacular a slice looks sitting atop the coloured plates. The top plate and watermelon can be removed once everyone sits down, and put aside to be enjoyed for dessert.

Silver spoons with mosaic-style patterns reminiscent of azulejos or Mexican tiles find their perfect spot on a festive table. Or even

A mosaic of exuberant colours and hand-crafted accessories define Mexican style.

cutlery with brightly-coloured handles would look equally great; or a combination of mixed plastic ware would be perfect, depending on the menu and age of the children that will be present.

Scattered throughout the table are bougainvillea flowers and little plants and cacti in decorative mosaic-style candle holders. Both are typical Mexican plants but use what is readily available and what enhances your dominant colours. Brightly-hued, artisan-style small containers also hold toothpicks, plants, napkins—anything fun and unexpected. Even a Balinese tray blends in harmoniously as a tortilla chip server since it adheres to the colour palette and artisanal style of the setting.

No Mexican-themed child's birthday party would be complete without a piñata. This papier-mâché figurine, most often in the shape of an animal or star, is filled with candy and small toys and swung at by the party guests until it is broken and the contents come flying down to the ground. Piñatas can be found in many party supply stores but they are also not difficult to make at home (instructions can be found on the Internet) and would be an exciting project to do with the children.

For a child's party, you will certainly have your work cut out in keeping the kids entertained and the adults relaxed. Keep things simple with the table and let the vibrant colours take centre stage.

A colourful piñata provides plenty of fun for all.

A brightly coloured wooden puzzle in the shape of a cactus seems all too appropriate to not include in the decorations. Take a look through your child's toy box—you might be surprised and inspired by what you find!

Rainbow-coloured fairy lights and a small Mexican ornament add a touch of whimsy to the fiesta.

Watermelon is not only delicious 'kid food' but it also holds a special significance in Mexico where it is unofficially the national fruit due to its red, green and white colouring, just like the Mexican flag.

Celebrating birthdays is a popular tradition around the world. Dating back to pagan times, it was believed that evil spirits were more dangerous to people when they experienced a change to their daily lives, such as turning a year older. Consequently, it became customary for the birthday person to be in the company of friends and family, who surrounded the honouree with laughter and joy in order to protect him or her from evil spirits. Positive thoughts and happy wishes were bestowed upon the birthday person and if gifts were brought, it was considered a welcome blessing for the honoured individual.

Eventually, birthday celebrations gained acceptance in all parts of the world, although countries celebrate in many different ways and place importance on different ages. In African cultures, the day a child is born is not observed as a special day. Instead, when African children reach a certain age, they are initiated into the community. In Japan, when a child turns three, five and seven, the occasion is thought to be especially lucky. In Korea, the 100th day after a child's birth (Paegil) is a day of celebration for the child's family. And in many Latin American cultures, a girl's 15th birthday (Quinceanera) signifies her passage into adulthood and the occasion is marked with a church ceremony, dinner and a dance.

Hand-painted ceramic animals make for amusing and useful table accessories.

Mexico is rich in artisanal traditions. Look for ways to incorporate these details such as with dessert spoons or serving utensils.

A Rustic Lantern Retreat
Mid-Autumn Festival

The natural beauty of wood is perfect for creating an inviting garden setting.

*Rustic, pared-down details look great when
teamed with a warm, grainy wood table.*

The moon cakes' round shape is a symbol of family unity.

Simple and chunky ceramic cups are dressed up with knotted greenery.

This Mid-Autumn Festival gathering takes a modern approach to an ancient Chinese celebration. At the centre of the festivities and of the table setting are moon cakes and lanterns. Taking a cue from the cakes' golden colour and the lanterns' rustic charm, the entire colour palette was intentionally kept neutral so as to enhance and not compete with their beauty.

The large teak table's faded patina serves as an ideal base for the low-key colour scheme. Each place setting is laid with round wicker place mats, wooden plate chargers and light coloured bamboo plates. Since the look is completely natural, even the simplest of chopsticks seem appropriate. Atop each plate, a beautiful moon cake greets guests. The metal holders cum napkin rings are perfect for displaying the moon cakes and for casually removing them before the meal begins. Although the cakes are usually served with tea as a light snack or an after-dinner treat, they are simply too pretty to keep hidden until later.

Grouping these wire lanterns creates maximum impact and make them a beautiful focal point on the table.

Jay the cockatoo looks on the festivities.

An unconventional yet completely appropriate centrepiece is a collection of old Chinese lanterns. Paper lanterns, wire lanterns and even the popular blow-up cartoon lanterns with music can all be used for decorating or for joining in the festivities.

Napkins, in the lightest shade of grey, are kept discreet in a tidy rectangle under the moon cakes. The only extra detail is the knotted greenery around the shapely ceramic tea cups. Long strips of greenery from the florist can provide countless opportunities for creative fun. Another way to use these versatile strips is to tie them around stemware, silverware or napkins, or simply add them to the table as squiggly touches of greenery.

It is not clear how moon cakes came to be associated with the Mid-Autumn Festival. One popular belief is that rebel leaders were planning an attack against their Mongol overlords on the day of the Moon Festival. In order to escape detection, they inserted secret messages in specially made round cakes telling all their supporters about the intended insurgence. On the night of the festival, they were successful in driving out the Mongol invaders and moon cakes have been a part of the festival ever since.

Moon cakes alongside antique moon cake moulds. Traditionally, 13 moon cakes were piled in a pyramid to symbolise the 13 lunar months.

The moon has been an auspicious symbol for many cultures since ancient times. For the Chinese, the custom of worshipping the moon can be traced as far back as the ancient Xia and Shang Dynasties (2000–1066 BC). However, it wasn't until the Tang dynasty in AD 618 that the Moon Festival gained popularity. The Mid-Autumn Festival takes place on the fifteenth day of the eighth month of the lunar calendar, the day that the Chinese believe the moon is the biggest, brightest and roundest. This day usually falls between mid-September and mid-October in the Western calendar. It is also a harvest festival—a special time to give thanks for a bountiful crop and for reuniting with distant family and loved ones. Of course, feasting, drinking tea, composing poetry and gazing and admiring the beauty of the moon are all part of the celebration.

At the centre of this festival are the beautiful moon cakes. Their round shape, like the full moon, is a symbol of family unity. Moon cakes are baked cakes between two to four inches in diameter, with a golden patterned pastry coating and a filling of red bean paste, lotus paste, date paste and/or other sweet meats. Nowadays, the fillings can become quite exotic and unconventional. It is customary to give at least one box of moon cakes to relatives and to enjoy them in each other's company.

Another symbol commonly associated with the Chinese, and more specifically this festival, is the lantern that children parade around with as a supreme totem of good luck and long life.

A Harvest Romance
French-inspired Harvest

A few subtle bundles of wheat discreetly convey 'harvest'.

A soft colour palette combined with floral details and fine china instantly asys romance and elegance.

Nobody does romance like the French. Combine this axiom with the ancient and worldwide tradition to celebrate a bountiful harvest season and all the makings for a romantic French Harvest meal have been planted.

By using a soft colour palette, and maximising the curves and mouldings of a pretty table and chairs, the mood becomes pure romance and elegance. With fresh flowers at each place setting, a large floral centrepiece was not really necessary. Why not create something equally stunning, practical and tempting for your guest? A cupcake, floral masterpiece, for instance. This grand centrepiece is actually quite easy to assemble. Place three cake

stands of diminishing sizes, one on top of each other and line them with paper doilies. Choose your colour palette and have fun. Cut the flower stems just before arranging them and they should last for the rest of the evening—a fabulous way to use roses that have already bloomed. Moreover, these flowers can often be obtained at great prices. For the place setting, look for uniquely shaped flowers or vegetables. The Brassica Oleracea is original in its resemblance to both a cabbage and a rose.

Don't be afraid to mix old and new; the look will be more contemporary and welcoming. Interweave your family heirloom china with inexpensive stemware; mix various floral designs on your

tea cups; combine real silver candle stands with acrylic and mercury-plated candle holders; mix coloured and clear crystal. As long as the colour scheme is consistent and the mood is romantic and soft, it will all come together smoothly.

Let the romantic, floral feel be your guide and you will be pleasantly surprised at how much inspiration can be found in the most unexpected places. These delicate sachets were too gorgeous to pass up and they make perfect 'thank you' gifts for your guests. Even small pill boxes will look right at home on the table and they can be used to hold some salt and pepper, or even after-dinner mints.

For as long as people have been planting, gathering and harvesting food, it is probably pretty safe to say that there has been some form of a Harvest Festival or, at the very least, a really great meal when the crop gathering was done. After all, a bountiful harvest is why the Americans celebrate Thanksgiving, the Chinese have their Mid-Autumn Festival, the Indians celebrate Onam and Pongal, the Africans have their Festival of Yams, and French Catholics celebrate the Feast of Saint Martin of Tours (also known as Martinmas).

In this day and age, many of us are probably not farmers, but it is certainly getting easier to enjoy fresh seasonal products from a good farmers' market. So wherever your inspiration may come from, the important point is to take the time to give thanks to nature's bounty and to enjoy it all with the ones you love. Say it with a memorable meal. Say it with flowers. Say it with your best china, stemware and heirloom pieces.

The welcoming glow of candlelight adds warmth to any table.

One truly special flower will speak volumes. The Brassica Oleracea is unique in its resemblance to both a cabbage and a rose.

Flower kebabs are another great way to use blooms that have already peaked. Simply insert them onto a wooden skewer with a few contrasting petals between buds.

The cupcake centrepiece.

Elegantly embroidered sachets are wonderful gifts that your guests will appreciate.

Be inspired by gorgeous floral shapes and blooms. Incorporate seasonal fruit, vegetables and flowers wherever you can.

Mixing different styles of silverware will give your table a modern look and your setting a casual but elegant feel.

menu

ons a la crème d'olives

s aux carottes epicees

e au citron et a la coriander

ourgettes au riz de camargue

pommes groseilles a la lavande

If you have the time, write out the menu. It adds just enough formality without all the fanfare. Additionally, simple place cards (made with small mirrors found in craft stores, some glue and glitter) rest casually atop a glass, and can be washed and reused for your next party.

A rose-shaped, decorative porcelain cup accompanies a fresh cut, cream-coloured rose.

An elegant dinner is the perfect time to bring out your best tea set.

Look for new and unexpected ways to display flowers. Why not use them instead of candles on an ornate candelabrum? As part of a side setting, it is an excellent way to extend the theme and dress up the surroundings.

Bollywood Lights
Deepavali

Lights, flowers, sparkles and colours combine to create an exotic Deepavali table.

Ganesh, the popular God of prosperity and wisdom, is surrounded by luscious Indian details.

It's all about colour, details, textiles and textures when you want to make an Indian-inspired table top. Here, to emphasise India's brilliant hues, vibrant shades of fuchsia and purples are set against a rustic teak table. Fresh banana leaves add another layer of colour and could even serve as the eating plate—Indian style. If fresh banana leaves are not available, a brightly coloured place mat, cloth or even patterned paper would add an equally great contrast to a dark table. The large, shallow dark bowls provide the perfect combination of modern rustic charm while also serving as ideal vessels for an exotic arrangement.

In the centre of each bowl is a decorated candle, fresh bird of paradise flower, silk flowers and richly decorated ornaments. Alternate and mix each setting for an extra colourful and opulent look. Plain purple, pink and gold candles are decorated with a glued-on clippings of Indian gods and trimmed with stick-on bindis. An easy effort with great impact! Before the meal, the tall candles can easily be placed along the centre of the table for an additional glow.

Be generous with all the elements. Being the Festival of Lights, you will never have too many candles. Use embroidered shawls, saris or scarves to dress the table or simply stack them in a side area for a visual treat. Place fresh flowers and garlands not only on the table, but use them to decorate the surroundings and even the chairs. No detail is too much as any Indian soiree should be a feast for all the senses.

Now is also the time to bring out any colourful and embroidered fabrics you may have stored in your cupboard. Top off your vibrant textile collection with flowers and a decorated fresh coconut (simply glue and twist colourful trimmings directly on to the fruit).

Inexpensive Indian glass bangles not only function as delicate napkin rings but can also be stacked to hold tea lights, candles or even a narrow tumbler, for an instant Indian vase.

Be original and creative with your light decorations. Bright yellow marigold petals and dyed fish scales surround a candle set atop a brass vessel. Coloured fish scales and delicate leaf petals can be found at local craft shops but your home also offers plenty of alternative possibilities e.g. rice, beads, coloured sand, glass pebbles.

A collection of superbly worked metal lassi cups placed with a few brass hand-painted ones plays up the Indian love of detail and richness of textures, while fresh banana leaves make stylish disposable place mats.

All it takes to transform candles into unique diyas are a few bindis, an eye-catching visual and a few silk flowers!

Use fresh flowers to enhance and adorn everything from tea lights strewn on the table to the dining chair. If there is an Indian neighbourhood in your town, you can probably find fresh garlands which make gorgeous additions to the festivities and serve as party favours.

A sari decorated guestbook is perfect for family and friends to pen their good wishes. Additionally, blue organza napkins are an indulgent but stunning addition to the table.

Each place setting is adorned with flowers and exquisite velvet ornaments in vibrant matching hues.

Deepavali. Diwali. Tihar. Hari Diwali. No matter how you call it, the Festival of Lights is celebrated with great enthusiasm and joy by Indians throughout the world. For five days in late October or November (Deepavali day always falls on the day of a new moon day), Indian households are brimming with family, friends, gifts, card games, lights, garlands and sweets as the entire family participates enthusiastically in this ancient festival of wealth and prosperity; and more symbolically, a festival signifying the victory of good over evil. It is also, according the Hindu calendar, the start of a new year.

The customs, rituals and story of Deepavali vary from region to region in India. However, they all stem from the epic Indian legend, the *Ramayana*. In the north of India, Deepavali day is celebrated to commemorate the day the wrongfully banished king, Rama, returns to his kingdom in Ayodhya after having won a battle and slain the evil Ravana who had kept Rama's wife prisoner. The rightful king regains his power and proceeds to be a great and noble ruler for many years. When Rama returns to the kingdom of Ayodhya, the entire populace turns out to welcome him in joyous celebration. There were diyas (small clay oil lights) everywhere to illuminate his way back home. In fact, 'Deepavali' in Sanskrit literally means 'row of lights'.

In Indian households, typically three activities are spread over the holiday. One is the wearing of new clothes and the *puja* or prayer at home which involves offerings of sweets, flowers, fruit, grain and invocations to the goddess Lakshmi (goddess of wealth) among other gods.

Secondly, the day before Deepavali (Dhan Teras) is considered auspicious to buy metal, so people buy steel or metal dishes for the kitchen as well as silver and gold jewellery. And lastly, the exchanging of gifts and the bursting of firecrackers and sparklers occur as a relic of the time when Rama returned and the entire city rejoiced.

Pumpkins A-Go-Go
Halloween

A warm blend of the contemporary still manages to evoke the ancient festival.

Allowing some of the table's surface to show makes the setting more interesting and helps to tone down a bit of the bold tablecloth.

If you want to create a refreshing Halloween table setting, resist the urge to go pure black and orange. In fact, if you go a bit retro and kitschy, you will have no problem mixing in plenty of fun Halloween decorations. By merging some orange plates with a bold patterned tablecloth, the look is American 1950s-, 1960s-retro meets Scandinavian chic. The light birch wood table and stools hold their own beautifully against the dominant tablecloth, while still allowing the black and orange place settings to shine. Melamine plates and graphic prints on glassware are making a comeback and for good reason—the style is practical and clean. Who wouldn't love that?

Centrepieces don't always have to be expensive. A black inflatable bowl serves as the perfect container for some fall weather gourds.

Or use any fruit or vegetable that is in season and it will not only be at its peak, but be quite affordable as well.

With the brightly coloured tablecloth, the feel is playful and cheeky. A few stick-on ghosts along the backboard and some friendly ghost candle holders lighten up the evening. Even a sprinkling of spiders will most likely entertain rather than horrify your guests!

The great thing about the mood of this setting is that the table is welcoming to young and old alike. Somewhere along the way, Halloween shifted from being a New Year ritual and medieval prayer ritual to becoming a favourite with children around the globe. But that's no reason for the adults to be left out of the fun!

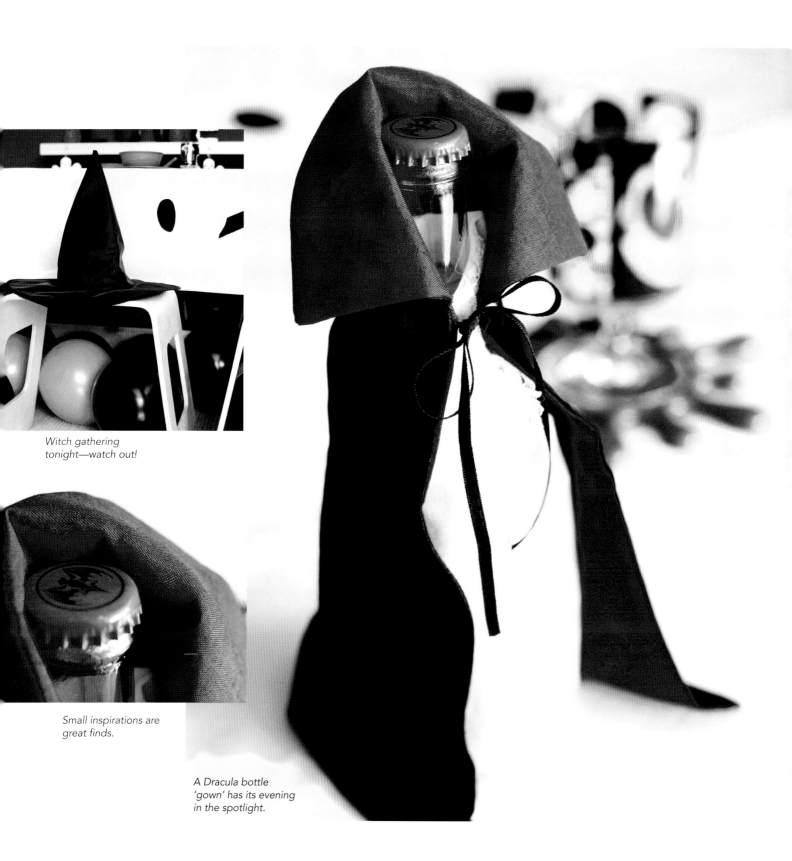

Witch gathering
tonight—watch out!

Small inspirations are
great finds.

A Dracula bottle
'gown' has its evening
in the spotlight.

Black melamine trays and plastic cauldrons add just the necessary touch of black to the table.

Creepy, crawly, sprinkled spider attack!

Decorate a few balloons with styrofoam letters for party fun.

Halloween is an annual event, celebrated on 31 October, primarily in the United States and Britain. The festival has evolved from many cultures, over many thousands of years. It grew out of the rituals of the Celts celebrating a New Year on 1 November in addition to the end of the 'season of the sun' and the beginning of the 'season of cold and darkness'. This New Year ritual was called Samhain (pronounced 'sow-en').

Then in the 1st century AD, the Romans invaded Britain and brought with them many of their festivals and customs. One of these was named Pomona which took place in October and honoured the Roman goddess of fruit and trees. The next influence came with the spread of the new Christian religion throughout Europe. In AD 835, the Roman Catholic Church would make 1 November a church holiday to honour all the saints. This day was called All Saint's Day, or Hallowmas, or All Hallows. Over the years, the customs from all these holidays mixed with 31 October and soon become known as All Hallow Even, eventually All Hallow's Eve, Hallowe'en, and then—Halloween.

The Halloween we celebrate today includes many influences—Pomona Day's apples, nuts and harvest; the Festival of Samhain's black cats, magic, evil spirits and death; and the ghosts, skeletons and skulls from All Saint's Day and All Soul's Day, the latter which commemorates the dearly departed.

Create a large dried flower arrangement for instant fall weather ambience.

All you need for a 'happy and spooky' Halloween.

Who could resist this trick-or-treater?

A Day of Celebration
Hari Raya Puasa

Decorating the home and preparing for visiting friends and family is an important part of Hari Raya Puasa. After the early morning visit to the mosque, most people will begin visiting relatives and friends. It's the ideal time to do a little extra to your table setting so you will be prepared to meet your drop-in guests with style and ease.

Play up the natural, inviting qualities of green (which is the dominant colour associated with the celebration and Islam in general) by combining it with yellow and gold. Not only is this colour combination warm and hospitable but it also gives you plenty of decorating options. For this high, narrow table, a trio of tall glass candle holders draws immediate attention to the setting while short stemmed sunflowers inserted in small pitchers create interest below. Individual tea and biscuit plates are laid out and accented with decorative *ketupats* (steamed rice cakes wrapped in coconut leaves that are traditionally eaten with a spicy meat dish during the festivities). Everything on the table is placed very simply, giving it a very warm, friendly feel.

To further enhance the mood, try to incorporate various textures—glass, wood and ceramics—in the same colour and embellish with intricate details. The natural bark of the cinnamon sticks is enhanced by the shimmery copper-tone glasses. Even a decorative garland of glass flowers along the table complements the colour scheme and softens the overall feel. The other secret for a festive home, of course, is to create interesting displays around your home, not just the table.

The popular Malaysian/Singaporean tradition of giving children *duit raya* or envelopes with money deserves a creative presentation of its own. Think vertically. Elegant bamboo sticks hold *duit raya* and *ketupats*. The latter can be made of ribbon or palm leaves when used for decorative purposes and can usually be found at Malay flower shops during Ramadan. Also, in keeping with the natural tones of the home, a few rustic jugs are perfect for displaying some gold branches in the hallway.

Spices make beautiful additions to the setting, and are practical too. Cinnamon sticks are not only handy to stir your tea with but also make for wonderful eye-candy.

Sunflowers add a dash of yellow and cheerfulness to the table.

An exotic display of textures, details and flowers make for an inviting and festive Hari Raya home.

Hari Raya Puasa, or Eid-Al Fitri in Arabic, is the biggest celebration in the Muslim calendar. This religious observance marks the end of the month of Ramadan, the ninth month of the Muslim lunar calendar and the holy month of fasting. 'Hari raya' in Malay means 'day of celebration' and the word 'puasa' originates from Sanskrit meaning 'fasting or abstinence', so taken literally, the phrase means a 'day of celebrating the fast'. It is also a time for worship and contemplation and for strengthening one's family and community ties.

Two of the main tenets of Islam are practised during Ramadan—fasting (Siyam) and giving gifts or money to charity (Zakat). Through fasting, Muslims believe that they can learn the principles of self-restraint and discipline that the Prophet Mohammed preached. This abstinence from satisfying their most basic needs and urges daily, from sunrise to sunset, is a form of worship and empowerment. Secondly, Zakat-ul-Fitr or the payment for breaking fast is collected from every family and given to charity.

Muslims in every continent celebrate and mark the end of the month long fast with prayers, large banquets, decorations, new clothes and gifts.

A vintage-looking flower garland adds delicate beauty to the table.

Decorating your lamp fixtures is another way to create a festive look and is easy to do. Tall glass candle holders not only add light and ambience but also instantly draw the eye to the table.

These green rustic jugs
are perfect vases for some
gold branches.

Ketupats can be made from ribbon for decorative purposes (usually found at flower shops during Ramadan), or fresh coconut leaves if encasing rice cakes. If you'd like to make your own, check the Internet for instructions.

Tall, simple bamboo sticks hold ketupats and also duit raya (money envelopes).

A simply laid table is perfect for drop-in guests.

A Mediterranean Miracle
Hanukkah

For this Hanukkah celebration, the inspiration is the Mediterranean Sea which borders Israel to the north-west. The sea's deep azure colour also recalls the Israeli flag. Be it winter or summer, the allure of the sea can be appreciated and enjoyed in numerous ways.

The dominant blue at the table comes from the mod acrylic chairs and the striking contrast they provide against the white tabletop. Blue is also used in the form of place mats, napkin rings, place card holders, blue starfish (these are naturally blue but even white ones could be painted if you so desire), blue and white graphic plates and a simple blue ribbon around the wine glasses. Individually, these are all small additions but together, they combine beautifully to create a seamless and polished table setting.

With the sea as your inspiration, a couple of large corals and shells are appropriate. More beautifully shaped seashells, in the form of a wind chime, adorn the tree and provides the perfect centrepiece to an afternoon lunch. Carry the sea theme further by adding a touch of whimsy to the place cards—sand. Simply use glue or Blu-tack™ to stick Scrabble™ letters to toothpicks, which are then inserted in sand to make fun name cards.

Overall, the look is very elegant and modern. Cloth napkins casually draped on each place setting blend with the appealing cutlery and wine glasses. In tandem, they play up the elegance and formality of the occasion while the laid-back ease of the nautical influence makes this Hanukkah meal the joyous, happy festivity that it has always been.

An elegant blue and white colour scheme pays tribute to the Mediterranean Sea and the Israeli flag.

Blue and white inspiration.

Seashells make perfect holders for salt and pepper.

Place cards always provide a great venue for creativity and individuality.

A seashell wind chime looks great and sounds even better.

A simple yet stylish place setting, as fresh as a Mediterranean breeze.

Hanukkah, or Chanukah in Hebrew, is the Jewish 'Festival of Lights'. Hanukkah celebrates the miracle of the oil that burned for eight days rather than one. The story goes that in 167 BC, the Greeks were determined to convert the world to their religion and customs. After seven years of conflict, a small group of Jews called the Maccabees defeated the larger and better equipped Syrian army. Upon their return to Jerusalem, they found their Holy Temple desecrated by the people they had just defeated. The valiant soldiers rededicated the Holy Temple but then discovered that there was only enough oil to light the menorah (candelabrum)—which is supposed to burn throughout the night every night—in the Temple for one day. Miraculously, the oil burned for eight days.

Hanukkah, meaning 'dedication', commemorates the rededication of the Temple, and is celebrated for eight days beginning on the 25th day of the Jewish month of Kislev. This usually occurs between late November and the early half of December on the Western calendar. The celebration is marked by the lighting of the Chanukah menorah, the playing of the dreidel or 'spinning top', the giving of Chanukah gelt or money to the children after the candle is lit and the eating of fried foods such as potato latkes and *sufganiyot* (jelly doughnuts) to celebrate the miracle of the oil.

Navy blue ribbon taped onto the wine glasses dresses them up for the occasion. One of the traditions of Hanukkah is that the entire family plays games. The most popular game is the dreidel, a four-sided top with Hebrew letters on each side. Each letter stands for one word from the phrase, 'A great miracle happened there (here).' Dreidels can be found in all forms, colours and sizes.

The lighting of the menorah carries great meaning and ceremony for the Jewish people.

Beautifully designed cutlery adds a modern flair to any table.

Build a rock pool in your own back yard. This large and low garden plant is ideal for holding a shallow bowl that has been adorned with starfish, rocks and floating tea lights.

The menorah has nine candles, with eight lined up in a straight row and an additional candle, the *shammash*, raised above the others. The eight lights represent the eight days that the day's worth of oil burned for and so it is forbidden to use the light of the menorah for any purpose, including to light a room.

As such, the *shammash* has been added so that it can be lit first and then used to light the other candles, going from left to right. On the first night of Hanukkah, one candle is placed in the holder on the far right of the menorah and then lit. On the following nights, one additional candle is placed to the left of the candle that was added on the previous night. This new candle is always lit first. The lighting ceremony is accompanied by blessings and ends with songs that highlight the miracle of Hanukkah. It is also common practice to place the menorah near a window or doorway to tell the world of the Chanukah miracle.

A cranberry-red centrepiece shines even
more when set against a modern, glass table.

We Wish You a Fairy Christmas
Scandinavian Jul

A delicate test tube mobile with red roses beautifully plays off the glass and red theme of the table.

If there is one holiday that is globally celebrated yet still manages to be closely linked to individual countries, it has to be Christmas. The food, the weather, the family traditions, the decorations— everything leaves plenty of room for interpretation. Although some elements may be firm family favourites, this holiday still offers plenty of possibilities for originality and creativity.

It's that magical time when families and friends get together, exchange gifts, feast on the family's best-loved dishes and rejoice for one's blessings. Why not take advantage of such a happy receptive audience and celebrate Christmas with a unique table setting that will bring smiles to the faces of young and old alike?

The inspiration for this setting comes from the exquisitely crafted Scandinavian fairies that make for a unique and memorable addition to the holiday table. Carefully displayed amidst red moss, pine cones and berries, these porcelain elves make a stunning centrepiece. And why not go a step further with the elf, fairy theme and make flying apples? To do this, simply carve a small hole in the apple to secure the candle, and hold the wings in place with decorative push pins. The candles' glow lightens up the dark, cranberry-red centrepiece and creates an inviting warmth.

If you have an original centrepiece in mind, work around it. Set it down on the table as your starting point and slowly work everything else in so as not to detract from the main focus.

The spicy scent and warm aroma of Christmas should not be overlooked. Beautifully displayed cinnamon sticks and incense elegantly enhance the fragrance and warmth of the festivities.

With all the detail and textures of the centrepiece, it is best to keep the rest pared down. A modern glass table provides the perfect base for a completely refreshing and contemporary look. Go ahead and play off the clean lines of the glass table and use more mirror and glass in the place settings. Four mirror tiles are pushed together to form the place mat and with the glass plates, your apple candle holders appear to be flying! An added bonus to using glass plates is that a decorative menu can be easily seen between the plate and apple decoration. Even small items such as the silver napkin rings help streamline the look by acting as name card holders. Matching coloured stemware completes the table. And if you do not have coloured crystal, fill clear glasses with a coloured drink for an extra special, holiday touch.

The idea is simple—take a traditional Christmas item and contrast it against a modern and clean background. The look is pure joy.

As a complimentary side arrangement or even as an alternative to the fairy centrepiece, take a few red glass containers, fill them with a generous number of thin candles and snuggle some red moss around the base.

Flying apples are in tune with the fairy theme, while glass plates allow for some fun to be inserted in unexpected places.

Apples are a favourite Christmas decoration in Scandinavia and are used in everything from wreaths to tree ornaments.

These Danish fairies are collected throughout the world for their beautiful porcelain features and life-like details in clothing and expression.

In the Christian calendar, Christmas is considered to be one of the holiest days of the year, celebrating the birth of Jesus Christ. Even though the exact date of his birth is not known, 25 December has been the given date for the celebration since the 4th century when the Roman celebration of Saturnalia (the celebration of the rebirth of the Roman sun god, Saturn) merged with the Christian celebration for their Son of God. In fact, the Roman festival of Saturnalia also contributed the merriment, lights and gifts to the Christian celebration of Christmas.

Today, as it was then, Christmas is a collection of traditions and practices taken from many cultures and nations. For example, the Christmas tree tradition is from Germany, gift-giving is from the Dutch tradition of leaving wooden shoes out for them to be filled with goodies and the yule log comes from Norway.

Every year, in the month of December, millions of homes all around the world are decorated with Christmas lights, candles and trees. This is Christmas, a time for carols, cakes, gifts and family gatherings. But most importantly, Christmas is also a time for sharing and for unifying.

By limiting yourself to only two colours, white and icy blue, the dramatic effect is greatly heightened.

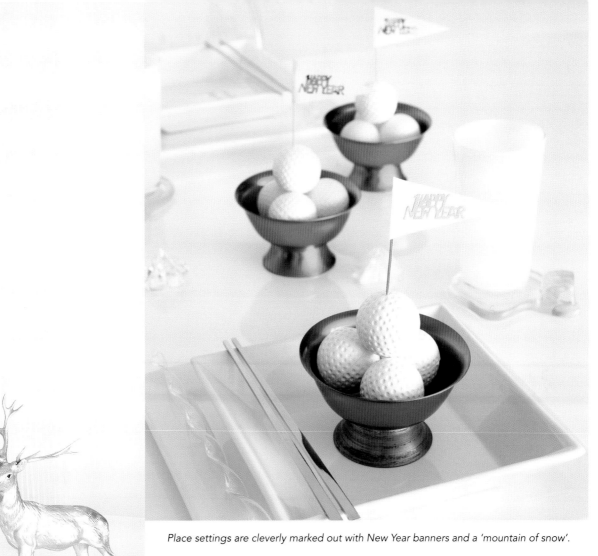

Place settings are cleverly marked out with New Year banners and a 'mountain of snow'.

Go north for this New Year's Eve theme. North, north, all the way to Iceland—think chilly weather, icy blue, cool silver and resilient reindeer. Guiding the décor is the illusion of ice and cold.

Should you ever find yourself in Iceland on New Year's Eve, you can join in this very popular celebration that, in certain communities, culminates in a huge display of fireworks and bonfires. They even have a popular myth that animals are able to speak like humans on New Year's night, and that elves and spirits move house!

This slick, white oval table is the perfect starting point for a 'cool' table setting. With the shiny surface resembling a block of ice and the transparent acrylic chairs beautifully enhancing the icy feel, the stage is set for a winter storm. A white tablecloth, some metallic material or even covering your table in tin foil would be equally effective. Sharp-lined square plates, frosty white glasses and individual blue metal saucers stacked with plastic golf balls to resemble a mound of snow cleverly stake the place settings. Of course, your menu will dictate the silverware you require but here,

we couldn't resist placing silver chopsticks-cum-ski poles.

The centrepiece is a few jagged twigs that have been spray-painted metallic silver and white, some silver Thai lotus bud sticks and glass icicles. What really counts here is the shape of what you use. Look for anything slender and textured as well as modern, asymmetrical and interesting. The other eye-catcher are the silver and white reindeer standing on small mirror decorations. They're unexpected and perfect for immediately conveying the arctic feel we are after. The reindeer look great alone, but by simply adding a few small mirror droplets under their feet, they become truly memorable.

Greet your guests with frosty glasses on a beautifully adorned tray and they will never want to leave the cold. Once you have a theme or idea for the celebration, it is easy to find clever and unique details that you may have simply overlooked before. It was hard to resist these plastic melted ice cube coasters.

And since it's a New Year's party, be sure to keep a few unexpected surprises till midnight. For instance, a lighted ice bucket, some sparklers and plenty of noise makers and confetti would do the job.

With such a fun theme and occasion, have your buddies dress in 'cool' colours, prepare a special menu or just enjoy the old favourites. Whatever your choice, delight in the company of your family and friends and the best is yet to come!

Look for clear or frosted glass, or acrylic hanging decorations. They are versatile and can be used the year round to enhance any arrangement or decorate a tray or side display.

A reindeer bell safety pin can be pinned onto anything for a bit of fun.

A herd of reindeer look surprisingly at ease on the table! A few mirror pellets add light and interest.

Mix special drinks to coordinate with your theme and to spread the colour and joy.

A drinks tray decorated with glass baubles and some wire garlands.

Just think of New Year's Eve as the great equaliser. Of all the holidays celebrated around the world, New Year's Eve (on 31 December) is the one that is currently celebrated in more countries than any other.

Not surprisingly, it is also the oldest holiday on record. New Year celebrations can be traced back to ancient Babylon over 4,000 years ago. Around 2000 BC, the Babylonian New Year began with the sighting of the first new moon after the vernal equinox (first day of spring).

Celebrating New Year's Eve on the last day in December can be traced back to the Romans when, in 46 BC, Emperor Julius Caesar began a new calendar. (Before this, the Romans celebrated New Year on the first of March.) Caesar's calendar is still in use all over the world today. The first month of January is named after the Roman god Janus, who is always depicted as having two heads—he looked backward on the last year and forward to the new one.

Interestingly, however, even for the many countries and religions

that do not use the Roman calendar, their New Year's is often marked by the movement of the moon, the position of the sun, or the sun and moon, harvest time etc. A new year still represents a time for celebration. It seems like the human soul searches to mark the end of the old and the beginning of the new.

New Year's is rife with customs, taboos and country-specific traditions. Feel free to incorporate as many as you like and don't forget to create some new ones with your family and friends.

Have plenty of sparklers on hand for the midnight celebration.

By sticking to two colours, the festive theme will be enhanced and the decorating will easily fall into place.

Keep plenty of votives and small decorative candles around. They add to the party and will encourage the festivities to continue late into the night.

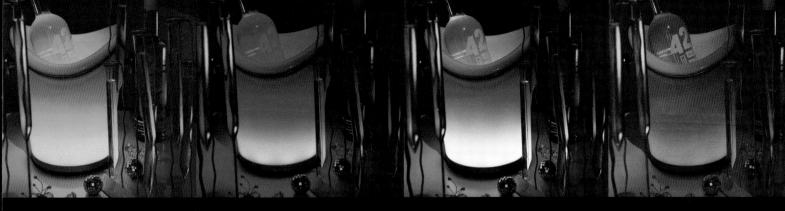

A lighted ice bucket is perfect for keeping the midnight drinks cold.

Traditions

- Don't forget to make a lot of noise to ring in the New Year. Not only do church bells ring worldwide at the stroke of midnight but people holler, horns blow and whistles ring through the night to frighten away evil spirits. In the northern hemisphere, it is also popular to light bonfires for the same reason.
- Make resolutions. There are records of the ancient Babylonians making resolutions (often in public) as a means for repaying any outstanding debts and returning anything borrowed was among the most popular.
- Sing 'Auld Lang Syne' by the Scottish poet Robert Burns.
- Using a baby to symbolise the New Year was started by the Greeks around 600 BC. It was their tradition to honour their god of wine, Dionysus, by parading a baby in a basket, representing the annual rebirth of that god as the spirit of fertility. The Egyptians also used a baby as a symbol of rebirth.
- Many people believe that what one does or eats on the first day of the year will affect the luck one would have throughout the coming year. Consequently, it has become common practice to celebrate the first few minutes of a brand new year in the company of family and friends.
- And along the same lines, traditional New Year foods are also thought to bring good luck. Many cultures believe that anything in the shape of a ring or circle is good luck because it symbolised 'coming full circle'. For this reason, the Dutch eat doughnuts on New Year's Day, the Spanish eat 12 grapes on New Year's Eve, and a handful of lentils is eaten at midnight in Latin America for good luck.

Small Touches,
Big Results

Now, the question is, how do I do this at home? Setting a beautiful table is so rewarding because it's possible to go from minimalist to maximalist and still achieve magnificent, creative results. If it's all too overwhelming or you just don't have the time, try to incorporate just one or two creative details to your table. You don't have to go overboard every time. Slowly gain confidence from your positive results and try to plan a little further in advance so you can incorporate more details and creative touches.

The first step, once you have the theme and occasion, is to choose a colour palette. Colour plays the biggest role in any table setting—it sets the tone. After your theme and colour palette are determined, the rest only depends on how far you want to extend these factors. The following are some points from my 'table-setting philosophy' that I hope will help get you inspired to create more global tables, regardless of whether you are a beginner or someone just looking for ideas.

- **Create memorable details**
  This is where a little creativity and extra effort goes a long, long way. It really does not take much to add a touch of whimsy and fun to any table. Many times, it is that simple fish crystal hanging on a glass stem that your guest cannot stop admiring. An original name card holder or even the ribbon around the every day glass can often make the biggest impression.

- **Utilise the extra potential of your chairs**
  Play around with the back of the chairs—this is an unexpected place for creativity and a great way to add some originality to your table setting. Chairs serve as perfect hangers so make use of this precious space whenever you can.

- **Be open minded when it comes to vases**
  With the myriad selection of gorgeous vases on the market, you would be hard-pressed not to find something perfect for the occasion. Many times, however, the ideal solution already lies in your own cupboard in the form of a coloured thermos, a small decorative bowl or even coloured glasses. When you are out and about, look for and collect interesting vessels that you find visually appealing. Keep them in a visible place and try to incorporate them whenever you can.

- **Think much more than flowers for your centrepiece**
  The centrepiece is the focal point of the table so save it for something spectacular. Of course a floral arrangement is the classic choice, for good reason; it's truly difficult to compete with the beauty of nature. However, even the perfect flower can be improved on when artistically presented in an original manner. For example, create lotus flower candle holders or place a couple of anthuriums with coal for drama and contrast. For a variation of this theme, instead of flowers use animals, red moss, candles, cacti, fruit, vegetables… The options are endless.

- **Look everywhere for inspiration**
  This is probably the most important and fun tip to any 'global table'. Explore ethnic neighbourhoods in your town or city, and when travelling, seek out stationary stores, party supply stores and small dime-store shops—these offer a plethora of inspiration and insight into new cultures.

- **Make inspiring 'compositions' for your surroundings**
  Extend your theme with a carefully thought-out arrangement on side tables, the buffet area or the entrance to your home. Group items based on colour, shape, material or even scale. A few unexpected touches—such as filling a beautiful tray with a collection of candles, burning a little incense, or hunting down a matador outfit—will reinforce your theme with surprising emphasis.

Acknowledgements

Thanks and appreciation to the following suppliers for their generous support:

Applecentre@orchard
t. (65) 6238-9378
www.applecentreorchard.com
IPods and accessories

Cyclo
t. (65) 9619-6059
Vietnamese lacquerware, paintings and lamps

D'Apres Nous
t. (65) 6733-5156
www.d-apres-nous.com
French, modern home accessories and more

FairPrice Antiques
t. (65) 9011-0380
www.fairpriceantique.com
Chinese furniture, lanterns, baskets and artefacts

Galerie Cho Lon
t. (65) 6473-7922
A collection of unusual books, recordings, furniture
and accessories from Asia and beyond

Good Value Imports
t. (65) 9295-7525
www.goodvalueimport.com
Vietnamese furniture, home and
garden accessories

LH Home Essentials
t. (65) 9690-8400
Danish design indoor/outdoor lanterns and
candle stands

Life Shop
t. (65) 6338-3998
www.thelifeshop.com
Home and fashion wear with a touch of
new Asia

Lim's Arts & Living
t. (65) 6467-1300
From ethnic splendour to
contemporary minimalism

Linen Deco
t. (65) 9835-7630
www.linendeco.com
Fine Belgian linen napkins, tablecloths and more

The Loft
t. (65) 6738-7687
Fine home accessories, glassware and more

Molecule
t. (65) 6733-2732
Cool and modern home accessories from Europe
and the United States

Olathe
t. (65) 6339-6880
Ethnic furniture and accessories from
South-east Asia and India

Originals
t. (65) 6471-9918
One-of-a-kind antique furniture from India
and Indonesia

Patient Care Centre
Tan Tock Seng Hospital, Singapore
Rose buds in various shades

Pdi Art Line
t. (65) 9853-0730
Visual artists for special events

The Shophouse
t. (65) 6344-0100
www.theshophouse.com
Recycled teak wood furniture in both contemporary
and classic designs

Space Furniture
t. (65) 6415-0000
www.spacefurniture.com
Australia's largest collection of
contemporary design

Takaraya
t. (65) 9796-8760
Japanese kimono, dolls, ornaments, tableware,
folkcraft and more

Ted Wu
t. (65) 6327-1241
Custom-made cushion covers

The Touch
t. (65) 6883-2239
www.thetouch.com.sg
Scandinavian home of design and art

Thank you to the home owners who allowed us into
their inspiring homes and gardens: Lone and Thomas;
Christine and Peter; Idrus and Jay; Liz and David; Ted;
Charlotte and Bill; Tony and Gerard; Linda and Mike;
Jens; Birgit and Henrik; Marión and Sanjay; Lynda and
Lloyd; Geri; Aloysius; Judy and Simon.

Special thanks to Marión for all your support throughout
the process of making this book and for your 'fab' way
with words, to Alan and Edward the best photographers;
to everyone involved in the project at Marshall Cavendish
International, especially Patricia, Lee Ming and Melvin,
to SPACE Furniture/Singapore for location, to Nathan,
Jens, Barbara, Linda, Marión, Conchita, Rebekka, Suede,
Nikolas, Spike and Jay for acting as models, to Judy,
Simon, Idris, Jytte, Kirsten and Svend, Caterina, Ali,
Jennifer, André, Cathy, Gitte, Mette, Sha, Siti Normah,
Rebecca, Joanie, Brian, Casey, Steven, Tina, and the
Spanish Tourism Board/Singapore for providing 'special
effects', to Alejandro and Gabriel, gracias from mamá,
to Jennifer for looking after the kids and finally to my
man Jens, for your patience and love.

Index

About the Stylist

Tatjana Schantz Johnsson is an interior stylist whose work appears regularly in a variety of magazines and newspapers such as *Home & Décor, Square Rooms, Wine & Dine, Harpers Bazaar, Home Concepts* and *The Sunday Times*. Part Danish part Faroese, Tatjana first earned a degree in Information Science and Librarianship in Copenhagen and London and next completed a diploma in interior decorating in New York. Tatjana has years of experience as a photo consultant at the picture desk for newspapers and magazines in Scandinavia. Her love for travelling has never left her long in one spot; she has lived and worked around the world from Nepal, Greece, Nicaragua to New York and London.

About the Writer

Chilean-born and U.S.-raised, Marión Bravo-Bhasin works as a freelance writer, concentrating on food and interior projects. With degrees in journalism and communications and a masters in international management, she started her career teaching in Africa before moving into public relations, advertising and marketing. She currently lives in Singapore with her husband and two sons.

About the Photographers

Working as a team, Edward Hendricks and Alan Lee have over a decade of experience in photography. They specialise in architecture, interiors and still life and their images have appeared in leading design and lifestyle publications.

From left to right: Tatjana, Edward, Marión and Alan.

EAT
rice